DONCASTER LIBRARY SERVICE

30122 01553842 0

COUNTRY INSIGHTS

MEXICO

Edward Parker

WAYLAND

COUNTRY INSIGHTS

BRAZIL • CHINA • CUBA • CZECH REPUBLIC • DENMARK • FRANCE • INDIA • JAMAICA • JAPAN • KENYA • MEXICO • PAKISTAN

GUIDE TO THIS BOOK

As well as telling you about the whole of Mexico, this book looks closely at the city of Puebla and the village of Celestún.

 This city symbol will appear at the top of the page and information boxes each time the book looks at Puebla.

 This rural symbol will appear each time the book looks at Celestún.

Cover photograph: Maria and Fernando del Angel, aged ten and eleven, at their primary school.

Title page: A basketball team from Celestún's secondary school before a game.

Contents page: People visiting the Pyramid of the Moon, at Teotihuacan.

Book editor: Alison Cooper
Series editor: Polly Goodman
Book designer: Mark Whitchurch
Series designer: Tim Mayer
Consultant: Dr. Tony Binns, Geography lecturer and tutor of student teachers at the University of Sussex.

First published in 1997 by
Wayland Publishers Ltd
61 Western Road, Hove
East Sussex, BN3 1JD, England

British Library Cataloguing in Publication Data
Parker, Edward
    Mexico. – (Country Insights)
    1. Mexico – Social life and customs
    – Juvenile literature
    I. Title
    972'.0835

ISBN 0 7502 2001 5

Typeset by Mark Whitchurch, England
Printed and bound in Italy by LEGO S.p.A., Vicenza

Picture acknowledgements:
All photographs, except page 34, are by Edward Parker.
Page 34: All-Sport Mexico (David Leah).

Map artwork: page 5: Peter Bull; pages 6 and 9: Hardlines.
Border artwork: Catherine Parsons

Contents

Introducing Mexico

Mexico is a country of great contrasts. It is the largest country in Central America. Within its borders, there are scorching deserts, snow-capped volcanoes and lush tropical rain forests. Mexico is also one of the twenty richest nations in the world, but, as in other Central American countries, there are big differences between the standard of living of the rich and the poor.

Long before the first Europeans arrived in 1519, Mexico was the home of some of the world's greatest civilizations. The best known of these include the Olmecs, the Mayas and the Aztecs. They built great cities and pyramids, and the remains of many of them can still be seen today.

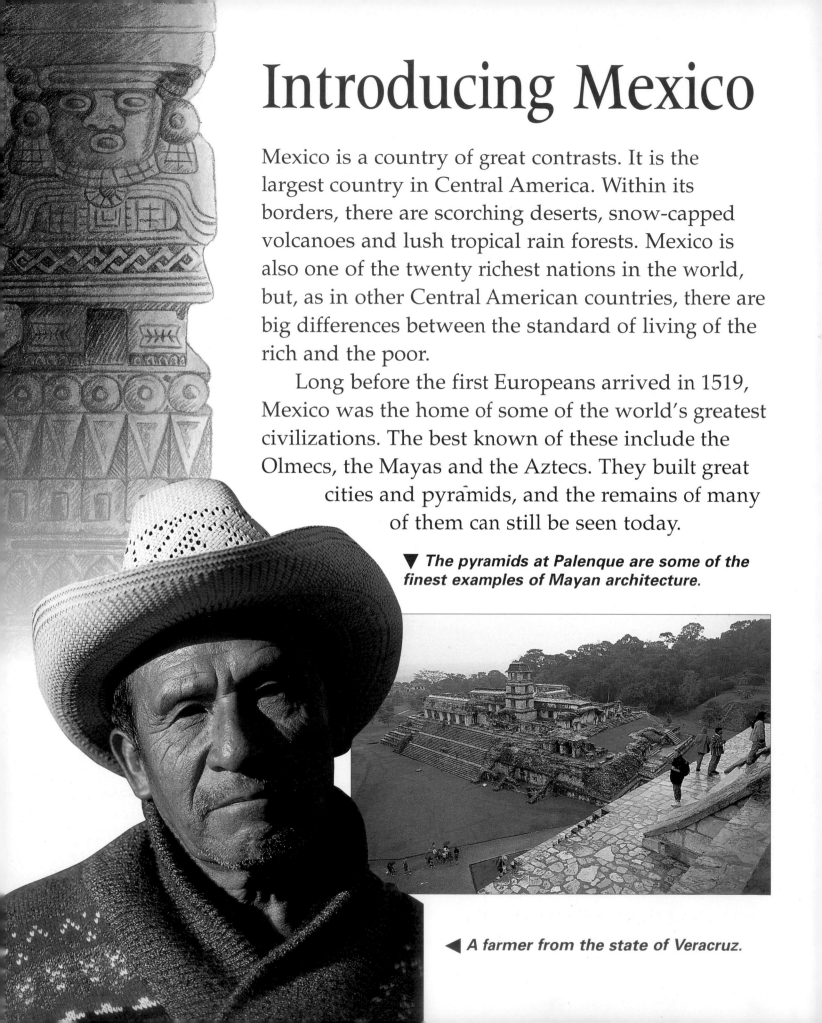

▼ *The pyramids at Palenque are some of the finest examples of Mayan architecture.*

◄ *A farmer from the state of Veracruz.*

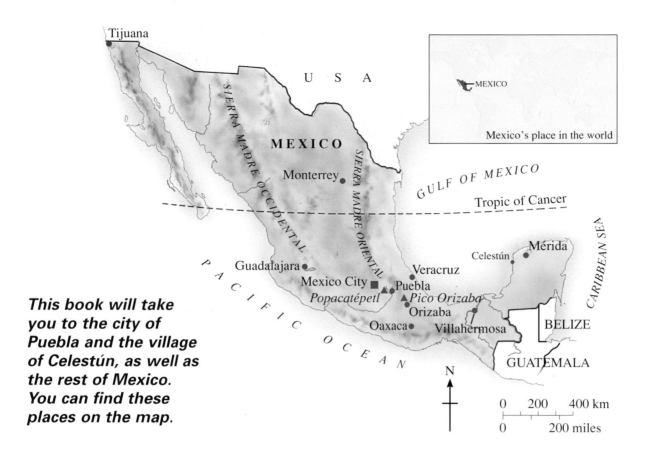

Mexico's place in the world

This book will take you to the city of Puebla and the village of Celestún, as well as the rest of Mexico. You can find these places on the map.

Mexico was conquered by Spain in the sixteenth century and Spanish rule lasted for 300 years, until 1821. The Spanish introduced Christianity to the country. Today, 90 per cent of the population are Roman Catholics. Spanish is also the main language. But many descendants of the great Mexican civilizations still follow their ancient religions and speak their own languages.

Mexico today is a highly industrialized country. The Mexican people are famous for their high spirits, their spectacular *fiestas*, and their spicy food, which is now enjoyed by people all over the world.

MEXICO FACTS	
Total land area:	1,972,547 km²
Population:	86.5 million (1993 estimate)
Capital:	Mexico City
Highest mountain:	Pico Orizaba (5,700 m)
Currency:	Peso

Source: *Country Profiles – Mexico 1994–5*, Economist Intelligence Unit

The city of Puebla

Puebla is a thriving city of over one million inhabitants, about 150 km away from the capital, Mexico City.

Puebla stands close to the site of an ancient Aztec city, called Cholula. Once, Cholula was an important city, but in the early sixteenth century, it was destroyed by the Spanish *conquistador* Hernán Cortés and his army. Puebla was founded a few years later, in 1531.

During the sixteenth and seventeenth centuries, Puebla developed into a wealthy city. It became famous for producing woollen textiles and painted tiles.

▲ *A view of one of the suburbs of Puebla.*

6

In 1860, the French army of Napoleon III invaded Mexico. On 5 May 1862, the Mexican army defeated the French in a battle at Puebla. There are reminders of this famous battle throughout the city – the main street, for example, is called the Avenue of Heroes. Every year on 5 May, *fiestas* take place all over Mexico to celebrate a great day in the country's history.

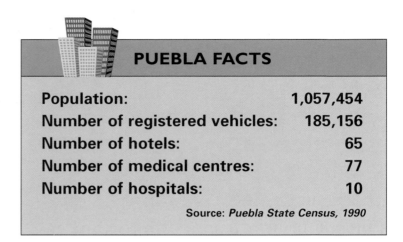

PUEBLA FACTS

Population:	1,057,454
Number of registered vehicles:	185,156
Number of hotels:	65
Number of medical centres:	77
Number of hospitals:	10

Source: *Puebla State Census, 1990*

The people of Puebla are a complicated mixture of the Nahua – who are descended from the Aztecs – and Europeans. Nine out of ten adults in Puebla speak Nahuatl, the Aztec language, as well as Spanish. Although the Nahua people tend to wear Western-style clothes for work, they still wear their own traditional dress for festivals.

A woman selling strawberries in the centre of Puebla.

The village of Celestún

Celestún is a large fishing village with a population of approximately 3,500 people. It lies on the coast of the Gulf of Mexico, on the Yucatán Peninsula. It is about 100 km from Mérida, the capital of the state of Yucatán.

The village is built on a narrow strip of land that separates the estuary of the River Esperanza from the ocean. Numerous sandy roads, lined with houses, branch off from the main street. Celestún does not have many old buildings, apart from the church. This is because the village has been destroyed several times over the last 150 years by fierce hurricanes.

▲ *One of the dusty streets in the centre of Celestún. Bicycles are the most popular form of transport in the village.*

Four young children from Celestún. ▶

Celestún has a limited number of services. There are three primary schools, a secondary school and a few shops. The medical centre is only open for a few days a week. Villagers have to travel to Mérida if they need to go to a bank or hospital, and the journey takes two hours by bus.

Celestún is in an area of Mexico that has a rich history. Over a thousand years ago, the Mayan people built impressive pyramids and cities in the forests of the Yucatán Peninsula. Links with this great civilization still survive today, as many people in Celestún have Mayan middle names and older people speak the Mayan language.

CELESTÚN FACTS

Population:	3,500 (estimated)
Number of medical centres:	1 (part-time)
Number of registered vehicles:	39
Number of hotels:	2

Source: *Yucatán State Census, 1990*

KEY TO MAP

	Houses
	Main road
	Tracks
	Beach
	Mangrove forest
	Salt pans

Land and climate

Mexico is a vast country, and it has many different climates. In the north, there is little rainfall throughout the year, and the region has cool winters and hot summers. This area is famous for its deserts and cacti. Much of the central plateau, where most people live, is over 2,000 m high. As a result, summer temperatures are cooler here than in the north. It has a temperate climate, with good rainfall, and these conditions are ideal for agriculture. The southern part of Mexico is tropical, with high temperatures and heavy rainfall throughout the year. Lush tropical rain forests grow in this region.

The main mountain ranges are the Sierra Madre mountains in the east and west of the country, and the transvolcanic mountain range. Mexico lies along a fault in the earth's crust, and so has had many earthquakes. In 1985, an earthquake hit Mexico City and 8,000 people died. The country also has many volcanoes, and some of them are still active.

▲ The snow-capped Pico de Orizaba, or Star Mountain, is Mexico's highest mountain. Its lower slopes are covered in dense forests.

▶ This cactus grows in Baja California, the driest area of the country, where only 50–100 mm of rain falls each year.

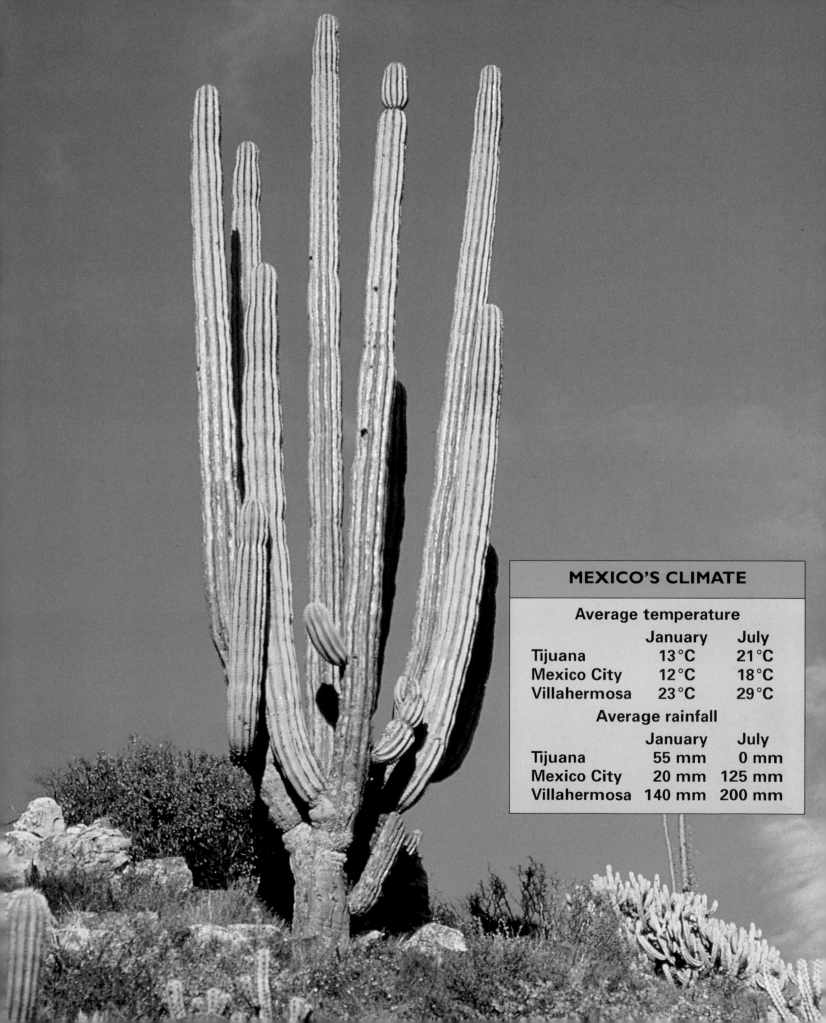

MEXICO'S CLIMATE

Average temperature

	January	July
Tijuana	13°C	21°C
Mexico City	12°C	18°C
Villahermosa	23°C	29°C

Average rainfall

	January	July
Tijuana	55 mm	0 mm
Mexico City	20 mm	125 mm
Villahermosa	140 mm	200 mm

Puebla's cool plateau

Puebla is at the southern end of the Mexican High plateau, at an altitude of 2,160 m. A chain of volcanoes, part of the transvolcanic mountain range, lie just 40 km to the south of the city. Several active volcanoes tower above the city itself. One of these is called Popocatépetl, a Nahuatl word that means 'Old Smoky'.

Puebla has a temperate climate, with good rainfall, and these conditions are suitable for agriculture. Like many Mexican cities, Puebla manages to combine agriculture with modern industry. Maize, beans and wheat are grown not far from factories producing chemicals, cars, textiles and electronic goods. There is a good local supply of clay,

The active volcano Popocatépetl can be seen in the distance in this view of Puebla.

which has provided the material for ceramic tiles and plates for several centuries. There is also a large construction industry that uses stone from local quarries.

▲ *A farmer and his helper on the outskirts of Puebla plough a field before planting a crop of beans.*

There are only two main seasons in Puebla: cool, dry winters and warm, wet summers. Even in summer, the temperature can drop quickly when it rains, and after sunset.

The winter months are dry, with warm days and cold nights, although it is not often cold enough for a frost. In and around Puebla there is a large traditional industry making woollen blankets and jumpers. On winter evenings, when the north wind is blowing and the temperature is only a few degrees above freezing, it is easy to understand why this industry has been so successful.

PUEBLA'S CLIMATE

Average annual temperature:	**16.7 °C**
Average annual rainfall:	**995.4 mm**

◄ *Winter mornings can be quite cold in Puebla and these children are wrapped up warmly as they wait for the school bus.*

13

Hot tropical coast

In summer, Celestún looks like a tropical paradise, with its long, sandy beach facing the calm green waters of the Gulf of Mexico. The temperature is regularly over 35 °C, but summer is also the season for heavy rains. Many days begin with clear, blue skies and end in a tropical thunderstorm. Several centimetres of rain can fall in an hour and the temperature can become pleasantly cool.

Celestún's climate makes it popular with Mexican holidaymakers, and foreign tourists have also begun to visit the village. They have been attracted by its beaches and the nature reserve, where there are pink flamingos, crocodiles and manatees.

CELESTÚN'S CLIMATE

Average annual temperature:	26.5 °C
Average annual rainfall:	777.1 mm

The main beach at Celestún attracts tourists from the city of Mérida at weekends.

For three months from mid-September, Celestún is at risk from ferocious tropical storms that develop out at sea. Occasionally, a storm develops into a hurricane. In 1995, two hurricanes hit Celestún. Many homes were destroyed and the whole village was flooded.

Winters in this area are dry, but there is sometimes a cold wind called *El Norte* (the North Wind). When this wind stops blowing, the temperature climbs quickly to more than 30 °C, and soon everyone is on the beach again.

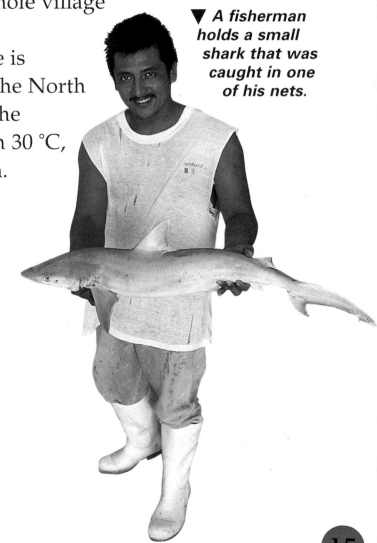

'In 1995, we had to leave Celestún twice because of Hurricanes Roxanna and Opala... We stayed in the football stadium in Mérida until the hurricanes had passed... When we returned home, we found that our house had lost its roof.' – Fernando del Angel, 11 years old.

Home life

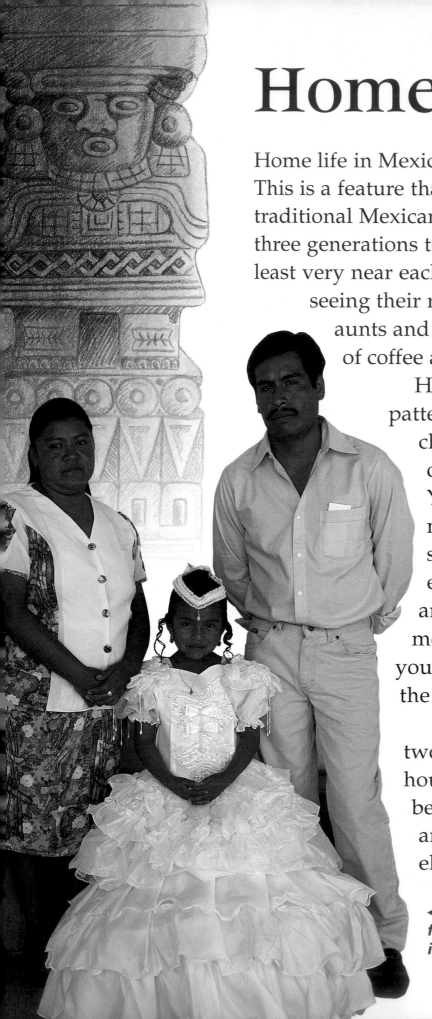

Home life in Mexico revolves around the family. This is a feature that the Roman Catholic and traditional Mexican religions share. It is usual for three generations to live in the same house, or at least very near each other. Mexican families enjoy seeing their relatives regularly, and uncles, aunts and cousins often drop by for a cup of coffee and a chat.

However, in recent years, the pattern of family life has been changing. The average number of children per family has fallen. Young men and women from many families have left home in search of work in the big cities, or even in the USA. In some villages and towns, the population is now mostly made up of old and very young people, because so many of the young adults have left.

In Mexican cities, a family with two children typically lives in a small house or flat, with one or two bedrooms, a living room, a kitchen and a bathroom. Most houses have electricity, a cooker and a telephone.

◄ *The girl in the picture is dressed for her first communion. Like most Mexicans, she is a Roman Catholic.*

In small towns and villages, telephones are rare, and firewood is the main fuel for heating and cooking. Baths are not very common in Mexico – most homes have a shower instead. A popular pastime at weekends is to visit thermal springs to bathe with the whole family.

▲ *Flats in a typical city street.*

Most Mexican houses do not have central heating. On cold nights, quilts or extra blankets are put on the beds for added warmth. In the hottest parts of Mexico, people often sleep in hammocks instead of beds.

▼ *This is a typical living room in a house in a Mexican city.*

THE *TORTILLA*

Most Mexicans eat *tortillas*, a type of pancake made from maize flour, with every meal. The traditional breakfast in rural areas is *tortillas* with meat, beans and chilli sauce. Filled tortillas, called *tacos*, are popular as a lunch snack in cities and in the countryside. Evening meals tend to be light – perhaps a couple of *quesadillas*, which are *tortillas* filled with cheese.

Home life in Puebla

There are a few blocks of flats in Puebla, but most of the houses are only two storeys high. This is partly because of the earthquakes that frequently hit the region, since lower buildings cause less damage than high-rise blocks if they collapse. The houses are usually built of brick or stone, and families live on one level, in flats. It is common for grandparents, parents and children to share the same house or flat or, like the Gomez family, to live next door or opposite.

Nowadays, many women have to do paid work to increase the family income, but they also continue to do most of the housework. They feel very proud to send their husbands and children out to work and school each day looking smart and clean.

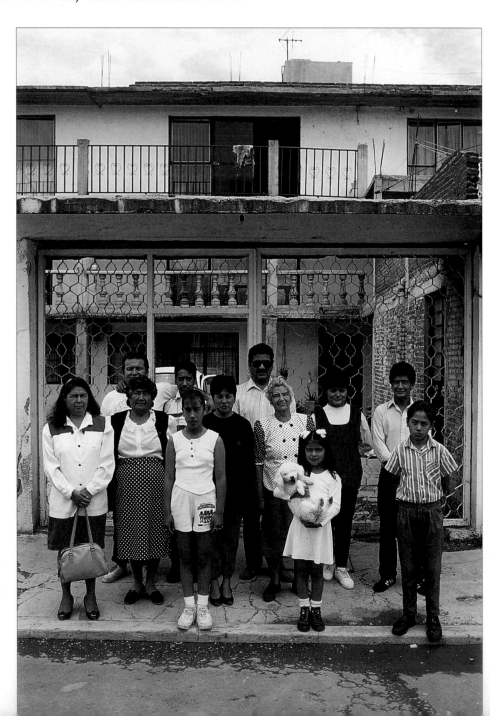

The Gomez family live in a house in Puebla. This picture shows them standing outside it, with several of their close relatives who live nearby.

18

Puebla is famous throughout Mexico for a special dish called *mole*. This is a sauce made from chocolate and chilli peppers, a mixture that has been popular since the time of the Aztecs. More than twenty other ingredients are also added and the sauce is poured over meat. It is the meal that is served on special occasions.

▲ Mole *is a special dish from Puebla.*

On most days, families eat their main meal together at about 2 pm. The children have finished school by this time, and most workers are beginning their *siesta*. Mr Gomez works long hours, and often the children are in bed by the time he gets home at night. The two-hour *siesta* in the middle of the day is a good opportunity for him to spend some time with his family.

▼ *The men of the Gomez family get together for the main meal of the day at around 2 pm.*

Like most Mexicans, people in Puebla usually have a late evening meal between 8 and 10 pm. This meal is lighter than lunch but still includes *tortillas*, meat, beans and chilli sauce.

Home life in Celestún

Most of the houses in Celestún have only one or two rooms. They are built of brick, or, more commonly, wood, and each is set in a small, sandy garden where fruit trees and other useful plants are grown. Families in Celestún are generally larger than families in the cities, and over the last few decades the population of the village has grown quickly.

The Pinzon family have a brick house, with just one large room in which they eat, watch television and sleep. There are no beds, but at night hammocks are hooked to the walls and strung across the room. Cooking is done in an outbuilding, which has an earth floor. Firewood collected from the local mangrove forest is used as fuel.

'There is only one doctor in Celestún and he is only here three days a week. If someone gets seriously injured, their family has to pay 200 pesos (£17) to hire a vehicle to take them to hospital in Mérida.' – Juan Manuel Pinzon, tour guide and fisherman.

Hammocks are the best way of keeping cool while sleeping because the network of cords allows air to circulate around the whole of the body.

▲ *The Pinzon children enjoy a meal of fish, crab,* tortillas *and beans after a morning at school.*

As Celestún is a fishing village, fish is on the menu most days. During the summer, the fruit trees in the garden provide plenty of oranges, mangoes and coconuts. It is a very healthy diet.

Most families do not have a car, but some of the wealthier families have a moped or small motor cycle. The most popular form of transport is the bicycle, and almost every family has at least one boat.

Sunday is an important day in the village because all the family have lunch and a *siesta* together.

▼ *Ellio Kaux Cauih Quintal uses his moped to visit the salt pans he owns. Ellio's first and last names are Spanish, whilst his middle names are Mayan.*

21

Mexico at work

People who live in the USA or Canada are likely to use something made in Mexico every day, although they may not realize it. Many well-known US and Japanese companies own factories in Mexico that make or assemble a wide range of products. These include cars, electrical goods, electronic components, furniture, chemicals and textiles.

It is cheaper for foreign companies to produce their goods in Mexico than to produce them in their own countries. Workers in the car-assembly factories, for example, are paid lower wages than workers doing the same jobs in the USA or Japan. However, conditions in these factories are usually good.

Many other workers are not so fortunate. Large numbers of Mexicans have to work long hours, sometimes in very bad conditions, for very low wages. Others work at several part-time jobs in an effort to feed themselves and their families.

The financial centre of Mexico City. The tall buildings are the offices of banks and other major companies.

A quarter of all Mexican workers are employed in agriculture. Mexico is famous for producing hot, spicy chilli peppers, avocados, tomatoes and many types of fruit. Fishing is also very important, and anchovies, tuna and octopus are exported all round the world.

Many people are employed in the oil industry, as Mexico is the world's sixth-largest oil producer. It is also the world's largest producer of silver. Other valuable metals mined in Mexico are iron, copper, lead and gold.

Mexico's natural beauty and its fascinating archaeological sites, such as the spectacular pyramids, attract millions of tourists each year. In 1993, tourism provided jobs for two million people.

TYPE OF WORK IN MEXICO

	Percentage of population (1990)
Services:	51%
Agriculture:	28%
Industry:	21%

Source: *Country Profiles – Mexico 1994–5,* Economist Intelligence Unit

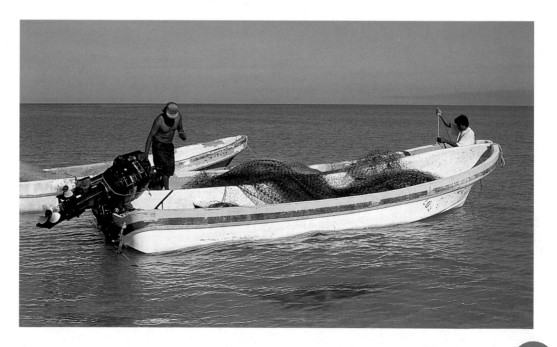

Fishing employs ▶ *many people in coastal towns and villages. These two fishermen are preparing to set off for a day's work.*

Work in Puebla

Many different kinds of work are done in Puebla. Factories produce everything from cars, textiles and chemicals to processed foods. In the centre of the city, there are banks and other financial companies. More than 50,000 Pueblans work for the local government, as teachers, administrators and doctors. Tourism provides jobs in hotels and restaurants. Visitors to the city are also keen to buy goods produced in the traditional way by weavers and potters.

TYPE OF WORK IN PUEBLA	
	Number of workers (1990)
Manufacturing industry:	88,000
Commerce:	58,000
Social services:	41,500
Construction:	21,500
Other services:	97,500

Sergio Gomez works as a taxi driver for one of the many co-operatives in Puebla. A co-operative is a business in which the workers own the company and share the profits between them. Mr Gomez works for five or six days a week, and usually for ten hours a day.

▼ *This man is using a loom to weave wool, which will be used to make jumpers.*

'I am learning all about electrical circuits at school. When I'm older, I want to work at the Volkswagen factory as an electrician, like my uncle.' – José Gomez, 13 years old.

Sergio's brother, Jorge, works at the Volkswagen factory on the outskirts of Puebla. This factory employs over 13,000 people – more than any other factory in the city. Most of the 950 cars produced each week are exported to the USA, although some are sold in Mexico. Jorge is an electrician, and he works a forty-hour week, in either morning or afternoon shifts. The working conditions are good, and there are clubs and other activities that employees can take part in once the working day is over. There is strong competition to get a job here.

José Gomez working on an experimental electrical circuit at home.

Work in Celestún

In Celestún, the range of jobs available is quite limited. Usually at least one member of every family is involved in fishing.

Juan Mex Quintal usually sets off to sea on Sunday afternoons and spends one or two nights away, depending on how good the fishing is. He cannot go out to sea in bad weather, and storms can sometimes prevent him from working for up to a week.

Juan delivers his catch to one of the fish-packing co-operatives on the beach. Here, the fish are sorted and packed in ice. Most go to the city of Mérida, but the more valuable fish such as yellow tail and lobster go to the USA. Octopuses are exported to countries as far away as Japan.

Near the village, there are several square kilometres of natural salt pans, and almost all the families are involved in collecting the salt from them. The salt is shovelled into containers and taken to Mérida to be sold.

Different types of fish are sorted and packed in ice at the fish-packing co-operative.

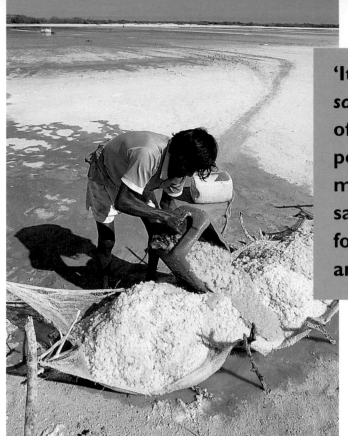

'It's hot work shovelling salt at the *salinas* [salt pans]... for each tonne of salt you get paid about 150 pesos (£13) but it does not take many hours to collect a tonne of salt.' – Ellio Kaux Cauih Quintal, former mayor of Celestún, shop and salt-pan owner.

◀ *A man working on the salt pans just outside the village.*

Tourism has developed quite recently in Celestún and has created more jobs in the few hotels and restaurants. Some people sell shells and other souvenirs, while others work as guides on the tour boats. Around fifty boats are used to take tourists to see the mangrove forests and the flamingos in the nature reserve. People who fish during the week can earn extra money by working as tour guides at the weekends, since that is when most of the tourists arrive.

This woman is selling the many ▶ different kinds of shell and coral found on the local beaches.

Going to school

Education is considered to be very important in Mexico. The government believes that it is vital to educate young people well, to ensure that the country will be successful in the future. Children are proud to wear the uniform of their particular school.

All Mexican children between the ages of six and fourteen are supposed to go to school. Almost all children enrol at primary school, which is divided into two levels, basic and higher. Each level lasts for three years. Unfortunately, in the countryside, many children leave before they have completed their time at primary school because they have to help their parents on their farms. Other children often have to look after the house and younger children while their parents are out at work.

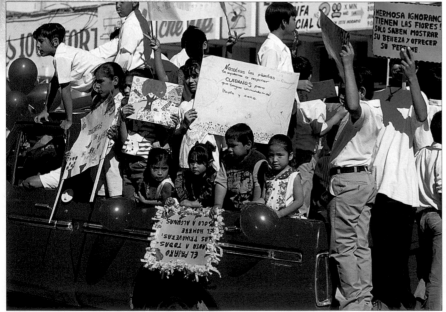

Children hold up banners asking for the protection of Mexico's natural environment.

EDUCATION IN MEXICO

In 1991 the average number of pupils per teacher was 30.

87.6 per cent of Mexicans can read and write.

In 1990, there were approximately 1.5 million students in higher education.

Only 60 per cent of pupils stay in education until they are 11 years old.

Over 50 per cent of children enrol for secondary education, for a minimum of three years. Those who want to go to college stay on for three more years, often at special preparatory schools. Pupils are given homework and tested regularly at this stage.

As in most schools around the world, lessons include reading, writing and maths. Mexican schoolchildren also spend a lot of time learning about Mexican history and environmental issues. Pupils are taught their rights and responsibilities as Mexican citizens, too.

Sport is considered important. Boys play football, baseball and basketball, while the most popular sport for girls is volleyball. Both boys and girls learn traditional Mexican dances.

MEXICO CITY UNIVERSITY

Mexico City University is the largest and oldest university in the Americas. It was founded in 1551 and now has more than 300,000 students. The students often have to take taxis from one lecture to the next, instead of walking, because the university is so large.

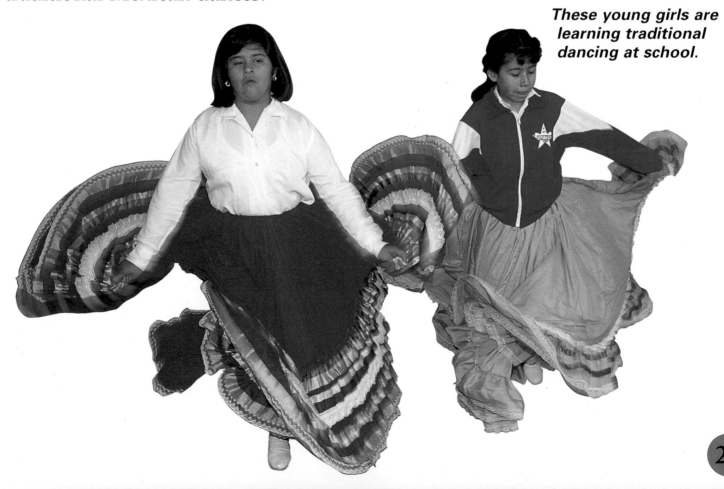

These young girls are learning traditional dancing at school.

School in Puebla

Puebla has 1,165 schools from nursery to secondary level. Between 7 and 8 am, the streets are full of children heading for school in spotless uniforms.

Ruben Ortiz is seven years old and he goes to the José Maria Lafrague primary school. Lessons include the history of Puebla and the geography of the local area. Pupils also learn what to do if there is a large volcanic eruption or if another earthquake hits the city. At some primary schools in Puebla, children start having computer lessons when they are about eight years old.

The two sons of Sergio Gomez attend their local secondary school. This is in one of the suburbs outside Puebla and the brothers walk there each day.

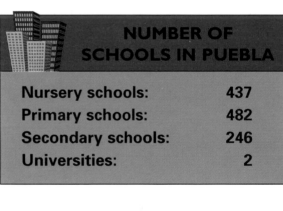

NUMBER OF SCHOOLS IN PUEBLA	
Nursery schools:	437
Primary schools:	482
Secondary schools:	246
Universities:	2

Ruben Ortiz in a reading and writing lesson at his school in Puebla.

Computer studies is the favourite lesson of these two children at the Instituto Garcia de Cisneros.

'We start the children on computers in primary school so that they learn to enjoy working with them... I would say that around 10 per cent of pupils at this school have a computer at home.' – Martha Salazar, Director of Instituto Garcia de Cisneros.

Omar is sixteen and is studying hard because he hopes to enter the famous naval academy in Veracruz. He knows that the entrance examination is very difficult. Omar's younger brother, José, has decided to study electrical engineering at school. He hopes to get a job as an electrician in the Volkswagen factory when he leaves school.

Puebla's two universities have very good reputations and students come from all over Mexico and from abroad to study at them.

School in Celestún

Celestún has a nursery school, three primary schools and a secondary school for children up to the age of fourteen. If students want to go on to college or university, they have to travel to Mérida, the state capital. The bus journey from Celestún to Mérida takes two hours, which is too far for students to travel every day. So they either live in college accommodation, or stay with friends or relatives during the week and travel home to see their families at weekends.

The school buildings in Celestún are much more basic than those in the cities, and there are not enough classrooms. The primary school buildings are used by one school in the mornings and a completely different school in the afternoons. Occasionally, lessons are held outside.

▲ *Pupils at Celestún's secondary school in the basketball team they have formed.*

A young girl learning ▶ about Mexican history in a Celestún primary school.

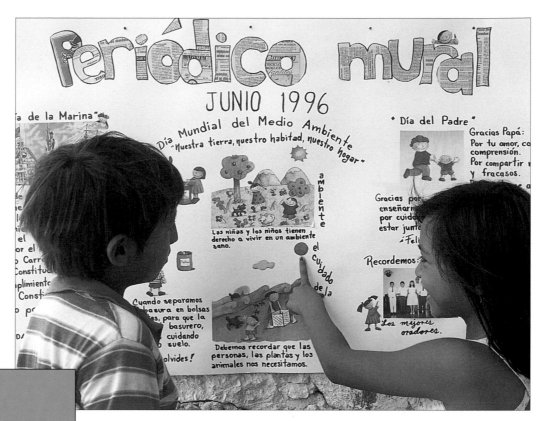

SCHOOLS IN CELESTUN

Nursery schools:	1
Primary schools:	3
Secondary schools:	1

'I am studying at the secondary school. I hope to go to a college in Mérida later. At the weekends, I earn money by catching crabs from the river.'
– Angel Guadelupe, 14 years old.

Children in Celestún do not wear uniform until they go to secondary school, but the younger ones are always smart and neat when they set off for school each day. As in all Mexican schools, the day starts with assembly. During assembly, some of the pupils parade the Mexican flag while the national anthem is sung. Children are taught to be very proud of their country.

The children spend most of their time learning reading, writing and maths. There is not much equipment to allow them to carry out science experiments, and there are no computers. Lessons about how to look after the local environment have started recently because natural resources are so important to the survival of the village in the future.

33

Mexico at play

Mexicans enjoy sport and *fiestas*, and they seem to have done so long before Europeans arrived in the sixteenth century. Near the Mayan pyramid of Chichen Itza, in the south of the country, there are the remains of a ball court with stone hoops on the walls. Here the Mayans played *ollamalitzli*, an early form of basketball, over a thousand years ago.

Today, the most popular sport is football, and almost every town and village has a team. At the weekends, people crowd into stadiums such as the Azteca in Mexico City to watch a match. Many people just play for fun in the parks or streets. Other popular sports are basketball, volleyball, baseball and rodeos.

IMPORTANT HOLIDAYS AND *FIESTAS*

17 Jan	Day of Saint Antonio de Abad
21 March	Birthday of Benito Juárez
23 April	Aztec Day
5 May	Anniversary of Battle of Puebla
16 Sept	Independence Day
12 Oct	Dia del Raza (Columbus Day)
1–2 Nov	Day of the Dead
20 Nov	Revolution Day
12 Dec	Day of Our Lady of Guadalupe

Mexico City's Azteca Stadium, one of the largest in the world, can hold more than 100,000 spectators.

There are many festivals in the Mexican calendar. These are usually held to celebrate religious days or major events in Mexico's history. Some, such as the Day of the Dead, are important for both Roman Catholics and those who follow the older traditional beliefs.

Music is important to Mexicans, and every weekend, *mariachi* bands can be seen playing music in the streets or at parties. Mexicans also like to dance, and many regions have their own traditional dances. At weekends, rock music is played in clubs and discos until the early morning.

Families enjoy getting together for parties. On warm summer evenings, entire families can be seen walking around the parks and plazas together, an activity known as *passeando*.

▲ *On national holidays and at religious festivals, Totanac Indians perform ritual 'flying'. Four men with ropes tied round their waists 'fly' from a 10 m pole. As they swing round the pole, the ropes unwind until the men land on the ground.*

▼ Mariachi *bands, like this one, play traditional Mexican music.*

Leisure time in Puebla

There is plenty for people of all ages to do in Puebla. It has most of the leisure facilities of a modern city, with shopping centres, cinemas, discos and night clubs. It also has many historic sites to visit, including the remains of the world's largest pyramid and the Loreto Fort, where the Mexican army fought the French in the nineteenth century.

▲ *The Agua Azul sports complex has a pool that is 5 m deep. It is built on one of the natural springs that well up throughout the city.*

José Gomez is described as 'football crazy' by his parents, because he spends most of his time playing in matches or practising with his friends. His older brother and his father also play for local teams. Puebla has a professional football team, too, and sometimes the whole family goes to watch a game in the city's 70,000-seater stadium.

◀ *Basketball is one of many sports enjoyed in the city.*

When the summer holidays arrive and the weather is hot, people crowd into one of the leisure complexes, such as Agua Azul. This has swimming pools, sulphur springs, playing fields and an amusement park. Puebla's many parks are also full of people walking and playing games, especially on Sundays.

In the summer, the Gomez family likes to go to one of the mountain holiday resorts where they sometimes spend a week in a rented cabin. Here, they can enjoy walking in the mountains, swimming in the rivers and breathing the fresh air. Another popular summer outing is to Africam, a safari park where elephants, lions and other African animals wander freely around the visitors' cars.

▼ *Omar Gomez enjoys watching television in his spare time.*

'In the evenings, after I have finished my homework, I like to watch TV or listen to rock music through my headphones.'
– Omar Gomez, 16 years old.

Leisure time in Celestún

Children spend most of their time out of doors in Celestún, because it is hot for most of the year. Football is just as popular here as everywhere else in Mexico. In Celestún, it is played in the dusty streets by young children and on the beach by the men who work in the fish-packing co-operative. Girls tend to play volleyball at school and in their spare time.

Most children are good swimmers. Some like to dive off the fishing boats moored by the beach and collect shells from the sea-bed. On Sundays and after school, Angel Guadelupe often goes out in a small boat to catch crabs, or small fish that his father can use as bait. Fishing provides him with some pocket money, which he spends on drinks or playing games in the arcade. Sometimes he goes to Mérida for a day out.

These boys are enjoying jumping from a fishing boat into the sea.

38

'There are not many things for children to do in Celestún, apart from ride their bikes, go fishing or swimming... There is sometimes a funfair in the town of Hanucuma [one hour away by bus].' – Juan Manuel Ucan Pinzon, 21 years old, tour guide.

José Luis enjoys climbing the fruit trees in his garden. He also has an unusual pet – a turtle. In the spring, thousands of turtles arrive at the beach to lay their eggs. Some of the eggs are collected and hatched by the villagers, who keep the baby turtles as pets until they are big enough to release back into the wild.

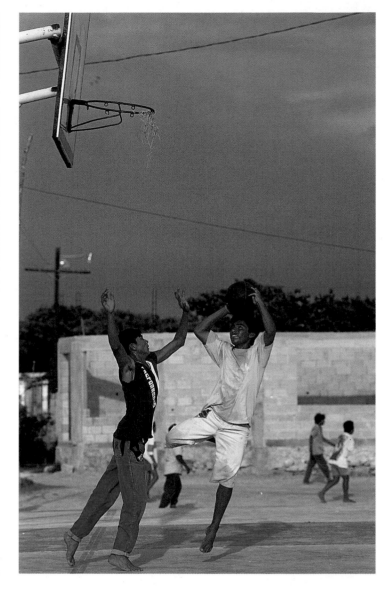

▲ *Two teenagers practise basketball on a Sunday afternoon in Celestún.*

◄ *Girls in Celestún like to play in groups. These girls are playing a card game, where they have to match the pictures on the cards to those on the boards.*

The future

Mexico has many things in its favour. It is one of the wealthiest countries in the world. It is rich in natural resources, such as oil, silver, timber and fish. It has a young, energetic population and a good education system. It also has a rich and powerful neighbour, the USA. All of these advantages give Mexico the potential to develop into an even wealthier and more successful country in the future.

However, Mexico faces many problems as a result of its large population and the growth of its industries. The population is expected to reach 100 million by the year 2000. Mexico City is one of the largest cities in the world, but scientists have predicted that it will be impossible for people to live and work there by 2020 because it is so badly polluted. Pollution is a problem for other cities too.

◄ *Mexico has many natural resources. This timber is from the forests in the state of Oaxaca.*

▲ *Thick, poisonous smog often hangs over Mexico City.*

Some of the richest people and companies in the world can be found in Mexico, but tens of thousands of people live in very poor conditions in shanty towns around the major cities. The government urgently needs to reduce this gap between the rich and the poor.

There are no easy solutions to the country's problems. But if it can tackle them successfully, the people of Mexico can look forward to a very bright future.

MEXICO'S GROWING POPULATION	
	(millions)
1970	48.2
1980	68.8
1990	81.3
2000	100 (estimate)

▼ *A shanty town in the city of Tijuana, northern Mexico.*

The future of Puebla

Dr Alejandro Dominguez uses these photographs of the volcano Popocatépetl erupting to help him in his work.

Puebla is a thriving city. It is likely to become bigger, and more wealthy. However, it may also face problems in the future.

There is a natural danger that threatens the city – the active volcano Popocatépetl, which began erupting again in December 1994. Within the first three days, 8,200 tonnes of ash had fallen on the valley of Puebla, and 33,000 people had to be evacuated. Fortunately, they were able to return after a couple of weeks. If there is a bigger eruption it would have more serious consequences for the city.

One of the worst problems facing Puebla is pollution. Fumes from vehicles and some of the large factories produce a poisonous smog that hangs over Puebla for most of the year. Many of the new factories, such as those that make electronic goods, cause much less pollution than the old ones. But Puebla will have to take action to reduce the pollution even more, as there is a danger of the city becoming seriously contaminated.

Over the last thirty years, new industries have been attracted to the city and have provided thousands of jobs. Despite this, many young people are leaving the area to seek better-paid work in the states of Quintana Roo and Baja California. Puebla needs to continue attracting new employment, to ensure that in future its young people choose to stay at home.

'Puebla will be the first factory in the world to build the new Beetle [car], from 1998. It is very proud to have been chosen.' – Beate Rueck, PR officer, Volkswagen Mexico.

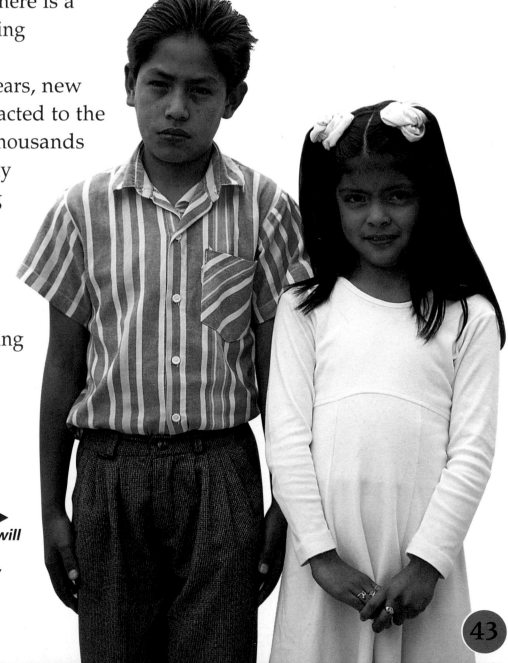

These two children, from the ▶ Gomez family, hope that they will find good jobs in Puebla when they are older, but that the city becomes less polluted.

43

The future of Celestún

Celestún's future will depend on its success in protecting the fragile environment around the village. Fishing is very important to the villagers but there are many more fishing boats than there were twenty years ago. If too many fish are caught, there is a danger that there will not be enough left to breed, and then there will be no fish for the villagers in the future.

The mangrove forests are very important to the survival of many fish. Large numbers lay their eggs there, and the roots give protection to the small fish until they are big enough to swim out to sea. However, the forest is very sensitive to pollution. An area near the village that is polluted with sewage and rubbish has already died.

Near Celestún, pollution has already killed some of the mangrove forest.

Tourism is important to the economy of the village, but this business could also be damaged if the mangroves and the rare birds and animals in the nature reserve are affected by pollution. The village needs better communications and improved systems for collecting rubbish and treating sewage to help it cope with the increasing number of visitors. Such changes would bring benefits not just for the tourists, but also for the villagers themselves.

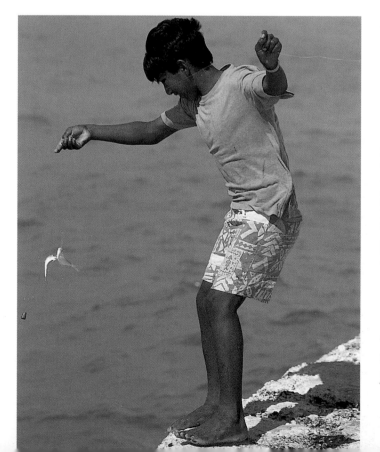

'After going to college in Mérida, many children return to Celestún, because they can earn a better living as fishermen than they can in other jobs in Mérida... Only a few children end up leaving the village for good.'
– Juan Manuel Ucan Pinzon, tour guide.

◄ Angel Guadelupe catches small fish for his father to use as bait. In the future he will probably become a fisherman like his father.

45

Glossary

active volcano A volcano that is likely to erupt.

altitude Height above sea-level.

conquistador A Spanish word for an adventurer or explorer who goes to conquer another nation.

contaminated Poisoned or polluted with chemicals or radioactivity.

estuary The area of a river where it widens as it reaches the sea.

fault A line of weakness in the earth's crust.

fiesta A Spanish word that means 'party'.

hammock A bed made of canvas or woven string, with cords at each end to allow it to be hooked up.

hurricane A storm with violent winds gusting at over 125 km per hour.

industrialized An industrialized country is one that has developed many industries.

manatee A large plant-eating mammal that lives in tropical seas around Africa, America and the West Indies.

mangrove A tropical tree that grows along coasts and has roots above the ground, rather than underground.

manufacturing The process of turning raw materials, such as steel, into goods, such as cars.

mariachi Bands of strolling musicians who sing and play guitars, violins and trumpets.

Nahuatl The language of the Nahua people, who are descended from the Aztecs.

plateau An area of high, level land.

resource A supply of something that people can use to survive or make money. Water, wood, coal and fish are all natural resources.

rodeos Displays of cowboy skills, such as bareback riding.

salt pan A shallow salt-water pool that forms after winter storms. The water dries out in the summer, leaving behind almost pure salt.

services Work such as tourism and banking, that involves providing people with facilities they need rather than making goods.

siesta A Spanish word for the long lunch break usually taken between 2 and 4 pm.

temperate climate A climate that has mild temperatures.

textiles Materials that can be made into cloth.

tropical climate A climate with high temperatures and rainfall throughout the year. This climate is found between the Tropics of Cancer and Capricorn.

Further information

Books to read

Country Fact Files: Mexico by Edward Parker (Macdonald Young Books, 1995)

Economically Developing Countries: Mexico by Anna Lewington (Wayland, 1996)

Focus on Mexico by Marion Morrison (Evans Brothers, 1994)

Look into the Past: The Aztecs by Peter Hicks (Wayland, 1993)

Passport to Mexico by Carmen Irizary (Watts, 1994)

A Taste of Mexico by Lynn Ellsley (Wayland, 1994)

What Do We Know About The Aztecs? by Joanna Defretas (Simon and Schuster Young Books, 1992)

VIDEOS

Video Plus: Exploration and Encounters (BBC Educational Publishing, 1993)

Useful addresses

Hispanic and Luso Brazilian Council, Education Department, 2 Belgrave Square, London SW1X 8PJ

Journey Latin America, 14–16 Devonshire Road, London W4 2HD

Living Earth Foundation, Warwick House, 106 Harrow Road, London W2 1XD

Mexican Tourist Office, 60–61 Trafalgar Square, London WC2N 5DS

Survival International, 310 Edgware Road, London, W2 1DY

World Wide Fund for Nature (WWF), Panda House, Weyside Park, Catteshall Lane, Godalming, Surrey

Index

Page numbers in **bold** refer to photographs.